Food Dudes

THE KELLOGG FAMILY:

Breakfast Cereal Pioneers

Joanne Mattern
ABDO Publishing Company

visit us at
www.abdopublishing.com

Published by ABDO Publishing Company, 8000 West 78th Street, Edina, Minnesota 55439.
Copyright © 2011 by Abdo Consulting Group, Inc. International copyrights reserved in all
countries. No part of this book may be reproduced in any form without written permission from the
publisher. The Checkerboard Library™ is a trademark and logo of ABDO Publishing Company.

Printed in the United States of America, North Mankato, Minnesota.
092010
012011

 PRINTED ON RECYCLED PAPER

Cover Photos: AP Images; used with permission of W.K. Kellogg Foundation
Interior Photos: Alamy p. 25; AP Images pp. 1, 4, 23, 27; Corbis pp. 5, 14, 18, 21, 22;
    Library of Congress p. 16; courtesy of Willard Public Library pp. 6, 8, 9, 15, 20;
    used with permission of W.K. Kellogg Foundation pp. 1, 7, 11, 13, 17, 19, 24

Series Coordinator: BreAnn Rumsch
Editors: Megan M. Gunderson, BreAnn Rumsch
Art Direction & Cover Design: Neil Klinepier

Library of Congress Cataloging-in-Publication Data

Mattern, Joanne, 1963-
  The Kellogg family : breakfast cereal pioneers / Joanne Mattern.
    p. cm. -- (Food dudes)
  ISBN 978-1-61613-558-4
  1. Kellogg, W. K. (Will Keith), 1860-1951--Juvenile literature. 2. Kellogg, John Harvey, 1852-
1943--Juvenile literature. 3. Kellogg Company--History--Juvenile literature. 4. Businessmen--
United States--Biography. 5. Cereal products industry--United States--History--Juvenile literature.
6. Breakfast cereals--United States--History--Juvenile literature. I. Title.
  HD9056.U6K456 2011
  338.7'664756092273--dc22
  [B]
                                2010027882

Contents

Battle Creek Boys

For more than 100 years, people around the world have been enjoying cereal for breakfast. Two brothers stumbled upon this breakfast revolution in 1894. Dr. John Kellogg first began experimenting with new ways to prepare healthy food. Yet, the younger W.K. Kellogg had a vision for the future. He successfully turned dry cereal into a thriving business.

John Harvey Kellogg was born on February 26, 1852, in Tyrone, Michigan. His parents were John Preston and Ann Janette Stanley Kellogg. Mr. Kellogg was a farmer and Mrs. Kellogg was a teacher.

When John was about four years old, the Kelloggs moved to Battle Creek,

W.K. Kellogg created the famous Kellogg's cereal enjoyed by millions today.

Michigan. On April 7, 1860, John's brother Willie Keith was born. John and Willie had many brothers and sisters! Their parents eventually had 11 children. Mr. Kellogg also had six children from a previous marriage.

Dr. John Kellogg's interest in healthy food led to the discovery of flaked cereal.

The Kellogg boys were raised as members of the Seventh-Day Adventist Church. This church promotes helping others and living a healthy lifestyle. The Kellogg family followed a special diet. They avoided meat, sugar, and caffeine. These rules stuck with John and Willie as they grew older.

Hard Work

John and Willie got their start in business from their father, John Preston Kellogg.

Growing up in Battle Creek, John and Willie helped their mother at home. All the children got up early to work in the gardens. Then, they sold vegetables to people in town to make extra money.

John and Willie attended school when they had time. Both boys were smart. But, some of Willie's teachers thought he didn't understand his lessons. However, Willie simply had bad eyesight. He couldn't see the chalkboard!

Willie found his first success selling brooms.

Mr. Kellogg ran several businesses in Battle Creek. He owned a broom factory and a small grocery store. John started working in his father's broom factory when he was 10. Two years later, he left to work at a publishing company.

Willie started working in the broom factory at a young age, too. Then when he was 14, he left school for good. He took a new job as a salesman for the broom company. Willie was very successful at this job. As Willie aged, he grew to dislike his name. So he shortened it to Will. Eventually, he went by W.K.

The San

While W.K. spent his days as a salesman, John kept attending school. He was good at science, and he cared about helping people stay healthy. So, he decided to study medicine. John attended college in Michigan. Then he went to New York. There, he graduated from Bellevue Hospital Medical College in 1875. This made him a doctor.

In 1876, John became the medical **superintendent** at the Western Health Reform Institute. The Seventh-Day Adventist Church ran this hospital in Battle Creek. John renamed it the Battle Creek Sanitarium. It became known as the San.

The Battle Creek Sanitarium, as it stood in the late 1800s.

John thought that many people's medical problems were caused by poor diet. He believed simple, healthy, natural foods would help people stay healthy. So, the San served only these types of foods. Patients there ate whole grains, fruits, vegetables, yogurt, nuts, and other natural foods.

The San is no longer around. However, many of John's ideas about health and nutrition are still popular today.

Falling in Love

Soon after arriving at the San, John met Ella Eaton. She was visiting a patient there. Ella was a nurse, and her knowledge impressed John. He offered Ella a job at the San, and she accepted. While working together, they eventually fell in love. John and Ella married on February 22, 1879.

That same year, W.K. traveled to Texas to run a broom factory. However, W.K. soon grew tired of the broom business. He also missed his childhood sweetheart, Ella Osborn Davis.

W.K. returned to Michigan after just one year in Texas. After he got home, W.K. asked Ella to marry him. She said yes! The couple married on November 3, 1881.

W.K. and Ella were very happy together. They eventually had five children. Their names were Karl Hugh, John Leonard, William Keith, Elizabeth Ann, and Ervin Hadley. Sadly, William and Ervin died when they were very young.

Later in life, W.K. enjoyed spending time with his grandchildren.

My Brother, My Boss

When W.K. returned to Battle Creek, he needed to find a new job. John offered him a position at the San. So in April 1880, W.K. began working there as the business manager.

W.K. worked very hard at the San. He did all the paperwork and paid the bills. He even made repairs. John was a difficult boss. W.K. had to do whatever his brother wanted. He even had to shine John's shoes!

For years, W.K. never got a day off. He often worked 15-hour days at the San. W.K. went to work before his children woke up. Then, he came home after they were asleep. W.K. wanted to spend more time with his family. But, he had too much work to do at the San.

John (seated) *came up with many new products and companies at the San. W.K.* (standing) *worked hard to keep them all straight.*

A Great Mistake

Meanwhile, John had big ideas about how to run the San. He set up a food lab there for experimenting. With his wife and brother's help, he developed new health foods for San patients. The food had no spices, salt, or sugar. It was very plain to meet John's standards.

In 1894, John tried to find a new way to serve wheat. Some patients could not chew the hard wheat crackers he provided. So, the brothers began experimenting with wheat batter. They boiled it and rolled it out to create a softer food.

One day, W.K. and John forgot about a batch of wheat. It sat out until it went stale. When the brothers later

John used the strict rules of the Seventh-Day Adventist diet for his patients at the San.

Their mistake in the kitchen changed the lives of the Kellogg brothers forever.

discovered the forgotten batter, they decided to roll it out anyway. They expected it to turn into sheets of dough, like previous batches had. But instead, the batter turned into flakes.

W.K. and John decided to bake the flakes. The baked flakes tasted great! The Kelloggs realized they had invented a whole new breakfast food. At that time, most people ate heavy breakfasts of meat, eggs, and pancakes. But the wheat flakes the Kellogg brothers made were light and healthy. The Kelloggs called their new cereal Granose Flakes.

Cereal Makers

Patients at the San loved Granose Flakes. One patient named Charles W. Post was especially interested in the cereal. So, he learned how the Kellogg brothers made it.

Other patients wanted to continue eating Granose Flakes after leaving the San. This gave John and W.K. a great idea. In 1900, the brothers started a mail-order company to sell their cereal. They called it the Sanitas Food Company.

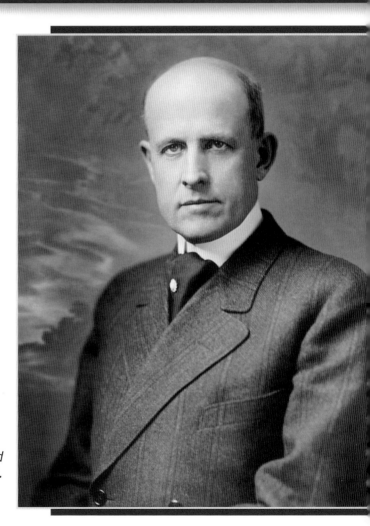

Charles W. Post founded Post Cereals in 1895.

In addition, W.K. wanted to advertise Granose Flakes. But John said no. John only wanted to sell it to San patients. W.K. was disappointed, yet he listened to his brother. W.K. worked hard to

make Sanitas a successful company. He sold 100,000 pounds (45,300 kg) of cereal the first year!

Meanwhile, W.K. also learned to make cereal flakes from other foods. Corn flakes were his next big idea. To improve the taste, W.K. added a little sugar. Yet when John found this out, he was very angry. He told W.K. that Sanitas products could not contain sugar.

W.K. invented the process for flaking corn in 1898.

Corn Flake King

Meanwhile, Post had left the San. Using the method invented by the Kelloggs, he created a cereal called Postum. Soon, he started his own cereal company. Unlike the Kelloggs, he advertised his cereals. By 1901, Post was a millionaire.

Post's success upset W.K. W.K. no longer wanted to follow John's rules. He decided it was time to strike out on his own. In

The Kellogg's Corn Flakes box has changed a lot over the years!

February 1906, W.K. started his own company called the Battle Creek Toasted Corn Flakes Company. He later renamed it the Kellogg Toasted Corn Flakes Company. Today, it is known as the Kellogg Company.

W.K. opened his first factory with just 44 employees.

W.K. was now free to run his business his own way. He made cereal with the ingredients he wanted. He also ran advertisements in magazines and newspapers. They were a big success. Soon, W.K.'s Corn Flakes were sold in stores all over the United States.

W.K. was so successful that other companies started copying his idea. They made and sold their own corn flakes. So, W.K. began labeling all the Kellogg cereal boxes with his signature. He wanted everyone to know that Kellogg's Corn Flakes were the original and the best.

Cereal Success

W.K.'s new business had a strong start. Then on July 4, 1907, his factory burned down. W.K. did more than rebuild his factory. He decided to include improved machines. Six months later, the new factory opened.

W.K. spent a lot of money so that people would recognize his company. He put up big signs to advertise his cereal. W.K. also gave away free samples. He even gave prizes to children who ate his cereal.

After his Corn Flakes success, W.K. continued inventing different kinds of cereal. He was always happy to try something new. In 1915, he introduced Bran Flakes. The next year, he created All Bran.

W.K.'s original (top) *and rebuilt* (bottom) *factories*

W.K. could produce thousands of boxes of cereal every day on his new machines. Today, that number is much greater!

Then in 1927, Rice Krispies came onto the market. People loved these options! The Kellogg Company did not stop creating famous cereals. Many are still sold today.

Family Lives

As W.K.'s company grew, he and John fought. Sadly, the brothers even stopped talking to each another. John stayed out of the cereal business. Instead, he continued his work at the San. In 1931, he opened another San in Miami, Florida.

John believed in a way of living he called the Battle Creek Idea. It involved exercising, spending time outside, and drinking lots of water. Today, we know John's ideas and healthy diet are smart advice. During his lifetime, John wrote nearly 50 books about health topics. He also edited a magazine called *Good Health*.

John followed his recommendations for health in his own life.

John and his wife weren't only interested in helping adults. They also had a strong interest in helping children. Together, they established an orphanage. They did not have any **biological** children. However, they cared for more than 40 children and adopted 12 of them. Their marriage lasted more than 40 years.

Sadly, W.K.'s marriage did not last as long. His wife was not well, and she died in 1912. Six years later, W.K. found love again. He married a doctor from the San named Carrie Staines. W.K. and Carrie spent many happy years together.

The Kellogg Manor House near Battle Creek served as a summer home for W.K., Carrie, and their family.

Giving Back

The Kellogg Company made W.K. a wealthy man. He used his money to help others. During the **Great Depression**, W.K. didn't want to take away anyone's job. Instead, he shortened work shifts at the factory. This allowed him to actually add more jobs.

Like John, W.K. also had an interest in helping children. In 1930, he started the W.K. Kellogg Child Welfare Foundation. Today, it is known as the W.K. Kellogg Foundation. At first, this group opened summer camps for Battle Creek children. Today, the foundation supports children in need around the world. It works to improve health care and education for them.

W.K. Kellogg

The W.K. Kellogg Foundation operates out of Battle Creek.

W.K. also cared about education. In 1932, he started the Ann J. Kellogg School in Battle Creek. He named it after his mother. Any child could attend this school, including those with learning or physical challenges. Special-education students learned alongside other students. The school was one of the first to do this.

In 1994, Kellogg College in Oxford, England, was named in honor of W.K. It serves adults returning to school to improve their lives.

Kellogg Today

Near his 80th birthday, W.K. was ready to retire. He remained on the **board** of directors until 1946. In 1974, Kellogg Company sales passed $1 billion. Today, Kellogg's products are sold in more than 180 countries.

W.K. knew he wanted the success of the Kellogg Company to benefit his foundation. So when he died, the foundation received a large portion of his **shares** in the company. The shares help fund many of the foundation's projects.

Both John and W.K. lived long, full lives. Yet they never reconnected. In 1943, John Kellogg developed **pneumonia**. He died on December 14 in Battle Creek. W.K. Kellogg suffered from heart trouble. He died in Battle Creek on October 6, 1951.

John and W.K. Kellogg were very different from each other. Yet together, they invented wheat flakes. With that cereal, the Kellogg brothers changed the way people eat breakfast. Today, the Kellogg Company is still a major food company. And, people still enjoy starting their day with Kellogg's cereals!

The Kellogg Company is the biggest cereal maker in the United States.

Timeline

1852	John Harvey Kellogg was born on February 26 in Tyrone, Michigan.
1860	Willie Keith Kellogg was born on April 7 in Battle Creek, Michigan.
1876	John became the medical superintendent at the Western Health Reform Institute, which he renamed the Battle Creek Sanitarium.
1879	John married Ella Eaton on February 22.
1881	W.K. married Ella Osborn Davis on November 3.
1894	At the San, W.K. and John accidentally invented wheat flakes; they called their new cereal Granose Flakes.
1900	The Kellogg brothers started the Sanitas Food Company.
1906	In February, W.K. started the Battle Creek Toasted Corn Flakes Company, which is known today as the Kellogg Company.
1930	W.K. started the W.K. Kellogg Child Welfare Foundation, which is now known as the W.K. Kellogg Foundation.
1943	On December 14, John Kellogg died in Battle Creek.
1951	On October 6, W.K. Kellogg died in Battle Creek.

Cereal Sensation

In the early 1900s, Battle Creek, Michigan, became known as Cereal City. The Kellogg Company was competing against more than 40 wheat flakes brands and more than 100 corn flakes brands made there! Today, Kellogg is one of just three cereal companies that remain in Battle Creek. The company's famous cereal brands have contributed to its great success.

Kellogg's Raisin Bran was first introduced in 1942.

In 1952, Frosted Flakes and Tony the Tiger made their debut.

Special K was released in 1956.

Corn Flakes was one of the Kellogg Company's original cereals. Yet, Cornelius Rooster didn't appear on the boxes until 1957.

In 1959, Kellogg's Sugar Pops were introduced. This cereal's name was changed to Corn Pops in 1967.

Apple Jacks were created in 1965.

The Kellogg Company purchased the Kashi Company in 2000.

Glossary

biological - connected by a relationship involving genes, rather than adoption or marriage.

board - a group of people who manage, direct, or investigate.

Great Depression - the period from 1929 to 1942 of worldwide economic trouble. There was little buying or selling, and many people could not find work.

pneumonia (nu-MOH-nyuh) - a disease that affects the lungs and may cause fever, coughing, or difficulty breathing.

share - one of the equal parts into which the ownership of a company is divided.

superintendent - a person who directs the work or operation of something. A superintendent may direct a group of workers, an institution, or a business.

Web Sites

To learn more about the Kellogg family, visit ABDO Publishing Company online. Web sites about the Kellogg family are featured on our Book Links page. These links are routinely monitored and updated to provide the most current information available.

www.abdopublishing.com

Index